MATH IT!
GRAPH IT!

by Nadia Higgins

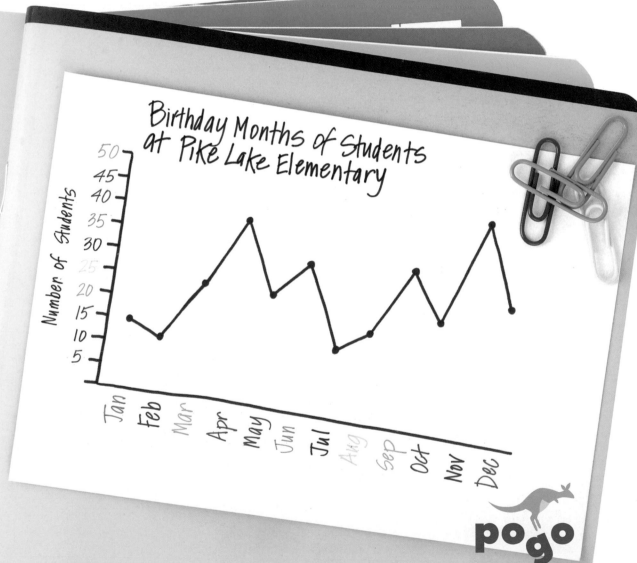

Birthday Months of Students at Pike Lake Elementary

Number of Students

50
45
40
35
30
25
20
15
10
5

Jan Feb Mar Apr May Jun Jul Aug Sep Oct Nov Dec

Ideas for Parents and Teachers

Pogo Books let children practice reading informational text while introducing them to nonfiction features such as headings, labels, sidebars, maps, and diagrams, as well as a table of contents, glossary, and index.

Carefully leveled text with a strong photo match offers early fluent readers the support they need to succeed.

Before Reading

- "Walk" through the book and point out the various nonfiction features. Ask the student what purpose each feature serves.
- Look at the glossary together. Read and discuss the words.

Read the Book

- Have the child read the book independently.
- Invite him or her to list questions that arise from reading.

After Reading

- Discuss the child's questions. Talk about how he or she might find answers to those questions.
- Prompt the child to think more. Ask: Have you ever read a graph? Was it easy to find the information you needed? Have you ever made a graph yourself?

Pogo Books are published by Jump!
5357 Penn Avenue South
Minneapolis, MN 55419
www.jumplibrary.com

Library of Congress Cataloging-in-Publication Data

Names: Higgins, Nadia, author.
Title: Graph it! / by Nadia Higgins.
Description: Minneapolis, MN: Jump!, Inc. [2017]
Series: Math it!
Audience: Ages 7-10. | Includes index.
Identifiers: LCCN 2016006413 (print)
LCCN 2016010660 (ebook)
ISBN 9781620314074 (hardcover: alk. paper)
ISBN 9781624964541 (ebook)
Subjects: LCSH: Graphic methods–Juvenile literature.
Mathematics–Charts, diagrams, etc.–Juvenile literature.
Classification: LCC QA90.H54 2017 (print)
LCC QA90 (ebook) | DDC 518/.23–dc23
LC record available at http://lccn.loc.gov/2016006413

Series Editor: Jenny Fretland VanVoorst
Series Designer: Anna Peterson
Photo Researcher: Anna Peterson

Photo Credits: All photos by Shutterstock except: Getty, 13, 14-15, 17, 18-19, 20-21; iStock, 5; Thinkstock, 8-9.

Printed in the United States of America at Corporate Graphics in North Mankato, Minnesota.

TABLE OF CONTENTS

CHAPTER 1
Read a Picture 4

CHAPTER 2
Get Ready to Graph 12

CHAPTER 3
Three Ways to Graph 16

ACTIVITIES & TOOLS
Try This! 22
Glossary 23
Index 24
To Learn More 24

CHAPTER 1
READ A PICTURE

What is the most common pet on your street?

What is the favorite lunch at school?

What sport do most kids play?

What makes you curious?
Chances are, you can graph it.

POPULAR STUDENT SPORTS

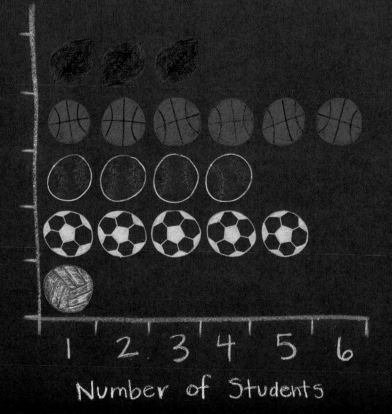

Number of Students

A graph is just a way to show information. Graphs use **symbols**, bars, and circles to show amounts. They are like pictures you can read.

So, what is the most common pet on your street?

Fish, by far!

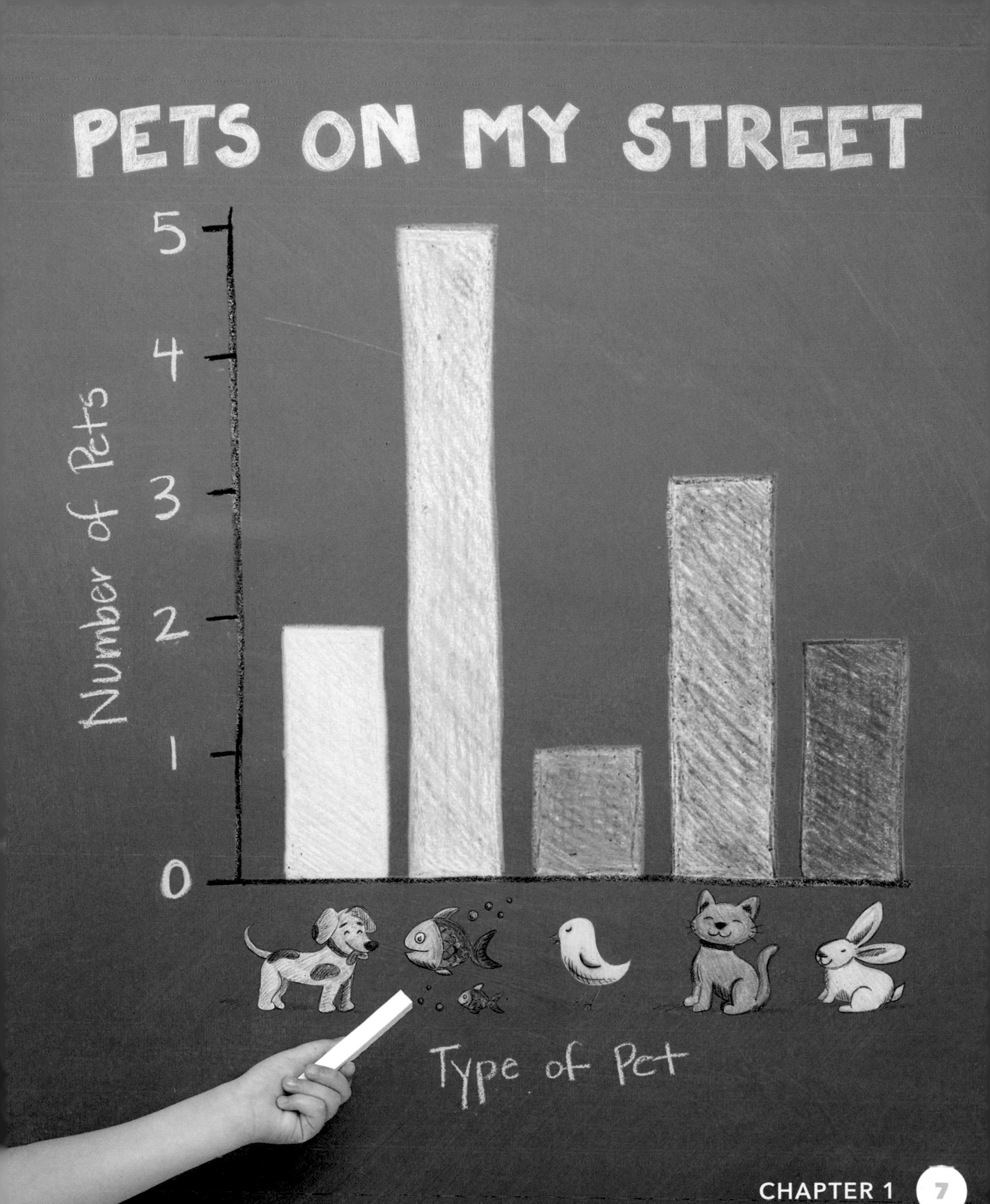
PETS ON MY STREET
Number of Pets
5
4
3
2
1
0
Type of Pet

What is the most popular
school lunch?

Looks like a tie between
tacos and pizza.

What are these kids doing?
Count how many go in each group:

- monkey bars
- ropes
- rings
- swings

What is the most popular activity?
You could figure it out from
a list of numbers. But a graph
shows the answer right away.

Just look for the longest
bar. There it is—rings!

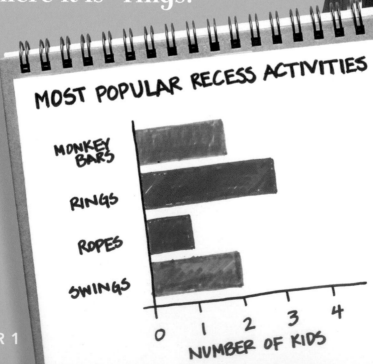

MOST POPULAR RECESS ACTIVITIES

	NUMBER OF KIDS
MONKEY BARS	
RINGS	
ROPES	
SWINGS	

0   1   2   3   4

CHAPTER 2

GET READY TO GRAPH

How do you make a graph? The first step is gathering **data**. This is the information your graph will show.

Pick Your Favorite Cake!
- ☐ Chocolate
- ☐ Vanilla
- ☐ Lemon
- ☐ Spice
- ☐ Red Velvet

Imagine your class is planning a party. Your job is to decide what kind of cake to serve. So you take a **survey**. You ask everyone to pick a favorite cake.

You give them a list of cakes. Each person votes for one cake. Use **tally marks** to keep track.

Draw one line for each vote. When you reach five lines, draw a slanted line across your straight lines. That makes a group of five. Then start another group.

Count by 5s to add up your tally marks. Add on any stray marks at the end.

Favorite Cake!
Chocolate: 卌 卌
Vanilla: 卌 ||
Lemon: ||
Spice: |
Red Velvet: 卌 |

tally marks

CHAPTER 3

THREE WAYS TO GRAPH

You have gathered and counted your data. What's the next step? Graph it! What kind of graph will you choose?

A **picture graph** uses symbols. Each symbol stands for a certain number. In this graph, each cake symbol equals two votes.

Favorite Cake!

Chocolate:

Vanilla:

Lemon:

Red Velvet:

Spice:

How many votes did chocolate get?
Find the **label** that says chocolate.
Count the pictures beside it.
Count by 2s to get 10 votes.

Look how the same data looks in a **bar graph**. How many votes did vanilla get? Look at the numbers going up the left side. The top of vanilla's bar lines up with seven. Vanilla got seven votes.

Compare your data in a **pie graph**. The whole circle stands for all the votes for all the cakes. Each slice stands for just one type of cake. The bigger the slice, the more votes that cake got.

Favorite Cakes in Ms. McCoy's Class

Number of students

10
9
8
7
6
5
4
3
2
1

Types of Cakes

Favorite cakes in Ms. McCoy's Class

10

1

7

6

2

Your life is full of graphing possibilities.

What will you graph next?

DID YOU KNOW?

Notice how every graph always has a title. That tells what the graph is showing. Can you find all the graph titles in this book?

ACTIVITIES & TOOLS

MAKE A PHOTO-GRAPH

Make a graph using objects in your home. Then capture your graph in a photo. Let's find out who has the most shoes in your family.

What You Need:
- one shoe from each pair of shoes in your home
- index cards
- paper and markers
- camera

❶ Check with your other family members. Is it okay if you play with their shoes?

❷ Gather one shoe from every pair in your house. Put the shoes in piles. Make one pile for each family member.

❸ Organize the shoes into lines, one line for each person. Try to space the shoes out evenly.

❹ Put one index card at the bottom of every shoe line. Label each card with the person's name.

❺ Use the paper and markers to write a title for your graph. Place it on top.

❻ Your graph is done! Take a picture. Who has the most shoes? Who has the least? What is another way you could compare the shoes?

GLOSSARY

bar graph: A graph that uses bars to show amounts. The taller the bar, the more it stands for.

data: Information that is shown in a graph.

label: A word that names the items that are being counted in a graph. Labels run along the bottom or side of the graph.

picture graph: A graph that uses picture symbols to show amounts.

pie graph: A graph that uses a circle with slices to show amounts. The bigger the slice, the more it stands for.

survey: A way of gathering information by asking a group of people the same question or questions.

symbol: A picture that stands for something else.

tally mark: A line that stands for one item in a count. Tally marks are useful when gathering data.

INDEX

activity 10

amount 6

answer 10

bar graph 18

bars 6, 10

cake 13, 14, 16, 18

circles 6, 18

data 12, 16, 18

information 6, 12

label 17

line 14

list 10, 14

lunch 4, 9

numbers 10, 16, 18

party 13

pet 4, 6

picture graph 16

pie graph 18

sport 5

survey 13

symbols 6, 16

tally marks 14

title 21

vote 14, 17, 18

TO LEARN MORE

Learning more is as easy as 1, 2, 3.

1) **Go to www.factsurfer.com**

2) **Enter "graphit" into the search box.**

3) **Click the "Surf" button to see a list of websites.**

With factsurfer, finding more information is just a click away.